THE BEST EVER JOBS

JOBS IN ENGINEERING

ROB COLSON

PowerKiDS press

NEW YORK

Published in 2023 by The Rosen Publishing Group, Inc.
29 East 21st Street, New York, NY 10010

Series editor: Amy Pimperton
Produced by Tall Tree Ltd
Editor: Lara Murphy
Designer: Gary Hyde

Cataloging-in-Publication Data
Names: Colson, Rob.
Title: Jobs in engineering / Rob Colson.
Description: New York : PowerKids Press, 2023. | Series: The best ever jobs | Includes glossary and index.
Identifiers: ISBN 9781725339132 (pbk.) | ISBN 9781725339149 (library bound) | ISBN 9781725339156 (ebook)
Subjects: LCSH: Engineers--Vocational guidance--Juvenile literature.
Classification: LCC TA157.C647 2023 | DDC 620.0023--dc23

Picture Credits

t-top, b-bottom, l-left, r-right, c-centre, fc-front cover, bc-back cover.
3tr and 30b shutterstock/Maria Kazanova, 3ct shutterstock/Lisses, 3cb shutterstock/researcher97, 3br and 31t shutterstock/ChickenDoodleDesigns, 4c shutterstock/Dn Br, 4b shutterstock/bioraven, 5tl shutterstock/ryanrafli, 5br shutterstock/Mertsaloff, 6bl shutterstock/motion.vidos, 7tr US Air Force, 7bl shutterstock/vector_brothers, 7b shutterstock/BORTEL Pavel – Pavelmidi, 8c, 9t and 31b NASA, 9b shutterstock/Drekhann, 10cl and 10b Design tech art, 11tl and 19cl shutterstock/bsd, 11br shutterstock/Kallayanee Naloka, 12bl shutterstock/Sergii Tverdokhlibov, 13t shutterstock/robuart, 13br Nadar, 14bl carlbob, 15t shutterstock/ I Wei Huang, 14cr Matt Brown, 15br shutterstock/angelh, 16b shutterstock/Fouad A.Saad, 17t Greater Vancouver Water District, 17br shutterstock/m.malinika, 18bl shutterstock Nadin3d, 19t unknown, 19b FMStox, 20c shutterstock/Keith Michael Taylor, 21t Amnesiac86, 21br shutterstock/vvushakovv, 22cr shutterstock/Rvector, 22br shutterstock/Lemberg Vector studio, 22bl shutterstock/defmorph, 23t PD-US-expired, 23br researcher97, 24bl shutterstock/Skocko, 24br shutterstock/Farah Sadikhova, 25tr shutterstock/Nikelser Kate, 25b shutterstock/drserg, 26bl shutterstock/NastyaSigne, 27t shutterstock/okili77, 28bl and 48br shutterstock/Perception7, 29t shutterstock/Tischa Ardis, 29bl shutterstock/Pan Xunbin, 29c shutterstock/Heiti Paves, 32c shutterstock/titi-kako, 33t shutterstock/Sergio Schnitzler, 33br shutterstock/WhiteJack, 34r shutterstock/Prokopenko Oleg, 35b shutterstock/Vector FX, 36b shutterstock/Constantine Pankin, 36br shutterstock/Skryl Sergey, 37t shutterstock/Kotkoa, 37b Getty/Bloomberg/Contributor, 38bl shutterstock/GabrielJose, 39t shutterstock/Adaptrographics, 39b AP/shutterstock, 40b shutterstock/dalish, 41t shutterstock/RGtimeline, 41b shutterstock/Elegant Solution, 42b shutetrstock/Anatolir, 43t shutterstock/MSSA, 43b Getty Images Entertainment/Tim P. Whitby/Stringer, 44b shutterstock/olllikeballoon, 45t David Dobkin, 45c shutterstock/Visula society, 45b shutterstock/good pixel.

Manufactured in the United States of America

CPSIA Compliance Information: Batch #CSPK23. For further information contact Rosen Publishing, New York, New York at 1-800-237-9932.

Contents

Top engineering jobs

Are you someone who loves to make things? Engineers are practical people who apply their knowledge of science and mathematics to real-world problems. Engineers work in a huge range of areas. They create materials, develop products, build new structures, or maintain computer and electronics systems. You could be working on the latest spacecraft or mending an elevator. Wherever there is a problem, there is an engineer on hand to fix it.

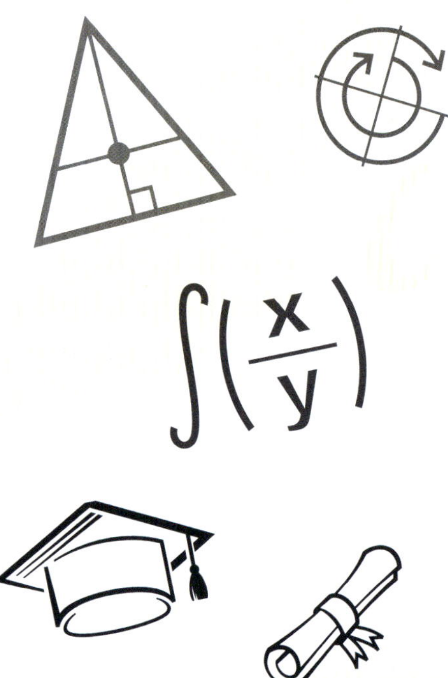

WHAT SKILLS DO YOU NEED?

Many engineers have a college degree. Practical solutions require accurate calculations, so you need to be good with numbers and have great computer skills. You'll also be working with industries right through your classes, giving you a great chance of a job at the end of it. After finishing your education, you'll have the chance to specialize in the area you're most interested in.

APPRENTICE OPPORTUNITIES

Apprenticeships give you the opportunity to learn on the job, instead of going to school. Over the course of a number of years, you'll combine study with work and earn a small wage as you do it. To win an apprenticeship, you'll need good math skills, so pay attention at school!

A DAY IN THE LIFE OF AN ENGINEERING STUDENT

A typical day for an engineering student involves a mix of classes and practical work. In the morning, you're likely to be brushing up on your math and science or learning new skills, such as computer-aided design (CAD). The afternoon is time for projects. For many students, this is the fun part: building and testing machines or models to try out their own ideas.

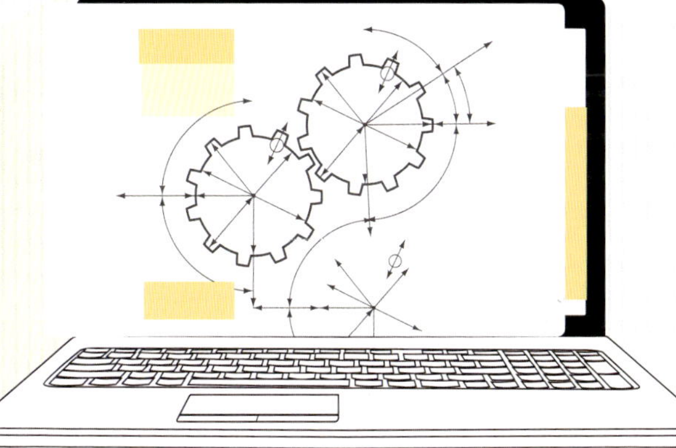

Aerospace engineer

Are you fascinated by flying machines? Do you marvel at how they work? Aircraft are incredibly complex machines and teams of skilled engineers are needed to build and maintain them. Aerospace engineers work on all kinds of flying craft, from helicopters and airplanes to unmanned drones and spacecraft.

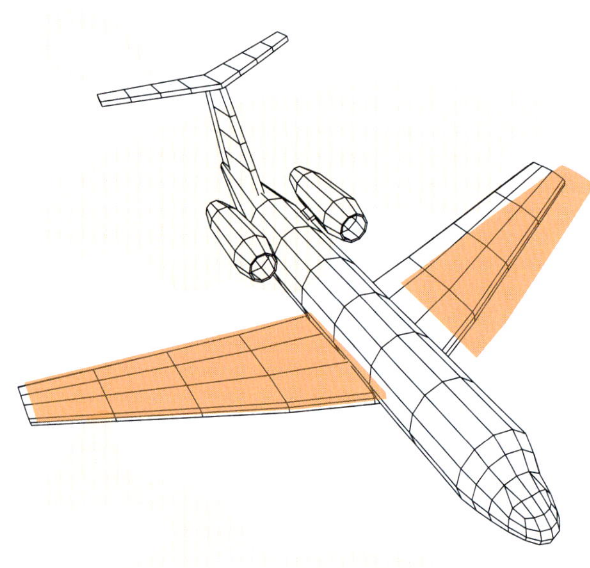

AIRCRAFT MAINTENANCE ENGINEER

Flying is one of the safest forms of travel, but accidents can be catastrophic. It is a maintenance engineer's job to make sure that a plane is safe before it takes to the skies. Mechanical engineers look after the engines and wings, while specialist avionics engineers take care of the complex electronic systems, including the autopilot, radar equipment, and control systems.

STEM STAR: MARY GOLDA ROSS (1908-2008)

In the 1950s, aeronautics engineer Mary Golda Ross put her amazing math skills to use on a top-secret project for the U.S. government. She developed new ideas for interplanetary space travel and wrote a handbook on the challenges of traveling to Mars and Venus. Ross's work was so secret that even her family did not know what she did, but later in her life, she was recognized by NASA as a space pioneer. A member of the Cherokee Nation, Ross was the first-ever female Native American engineer.

Ross worked on NASA's Agena rocket program.

SPACE ENGINEER

This is a job for budding rocket scientists! Space engineers design and build spacecraft. They may work in laboratories testing out new ideas or on-site, taking charge of rocket launches. A lucky few space engineers go into space as astronauts to work on projects, such as the International Space Station!

Behind the scenes: The Jet Propulsion Laboratory

Housed in a vast complex near Pasadena, California, the Jet Propulsion Laboratory (JPL) is NASA's largest research and development center and employs over 6,000 people. Here, teams of engineers develop and build the robotic spacecraft that are sent out to explore the solar system.

MARS ROVERS

Since 2012, engineers at the JPL's Mars Science Laboratory have operated the robotic rover Curiosity as it explores the surface of Mars. They communicate with the rover using radio signals, which take up to 24 minutes to travel between the two planets. The rover is equipped with a robotic arm and 17 cameras. It has sent back thousands of stunning images of the planet's rocky terrain.

NASA's Curiosity rover has been exploring the surface of Mars since it arrived on the red planet in August 2012.

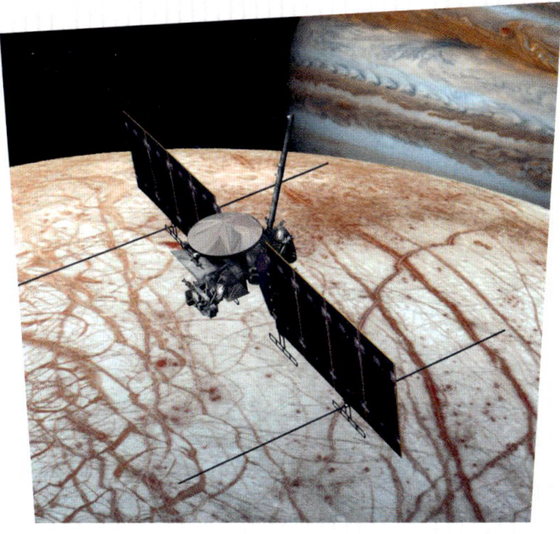

LOOKING FOR LIFE

Is Earth the only place in the universe with life? We don't know, but there are a few places in the solar system where scientists think life may exist. One of these is Jupiter's moon Europa. They think there is a deep, salty ocean beneath the moon's frozen surface, and it may support life. Set to launch in 2023, the JPL's engineers built the Europa Clipper probe. It will take a detailed look at Europa and its ocean.

The Europa Clipper probe may discover alien life swimming on Europa!

LONG-DISTANCE TROUBLESHOOTING

When a robotic spacecraft malfunctions, engineers have to fix it from Earth. Launched in 1977, the Voyager 2 spacecraft has flown past the planets Jupiter, Saturn, Uranus, and Neptune, and is now in the outer solar system. In 2010, Voyager 2 was 8 billion miles (13 billion km) away when it started to malfunction. JPL engineers successfully fixed its onboard computer by beaming up computer code to reset it.

Chemical engineer

Do you enjoy making weird-looking substances in the school science lab? If so, chemical engineering may be for you. Chemical engineers turn raw materials into useful products, and they may be involved in making all kinds of things, such as food, plastics, or drugs.

LAB WORK

Chemical engineers spend their time in laboratories creating new materials. They then develop practical ideas for manufacturing those materials on a large scale in factories. Many chemical engineers specialize in producing polymers. These are chemicals made from long molecules containing linked carbon atoms. Many of the most important human-made substances—such as plastics—are polymers.

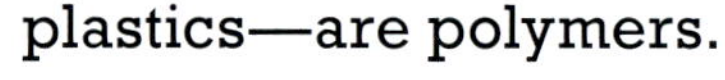

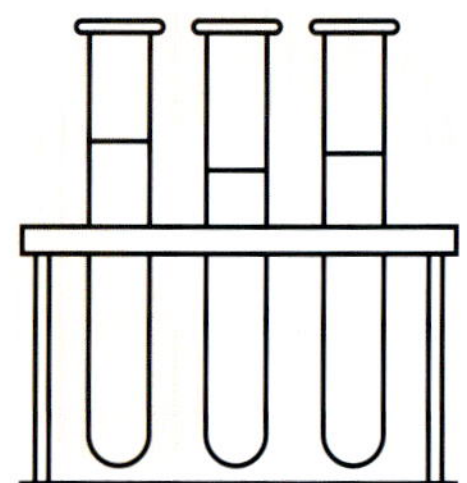

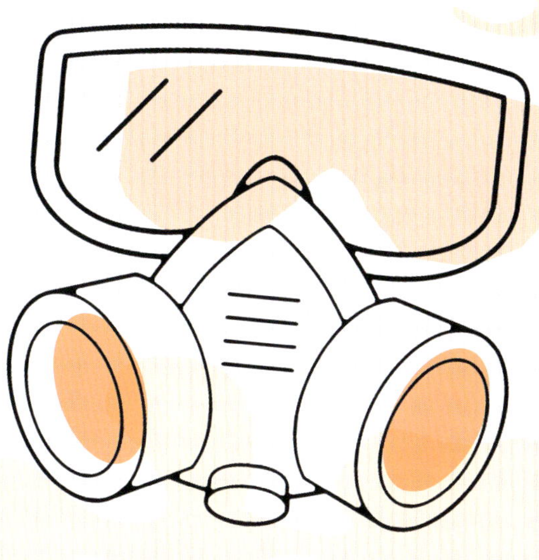

KEEPING SAFE

As well as working in the lab, chemical engineers spend lots of time in factories, designing and operating the machinery needed to make different materials. Chemical factories are often very dangerous places and one of the most important roles for a chemical engineer is to make sure that everything is being done safely.

STEM STAR: MARGARET HUTCHINSON ROUSSEAU (1910–2000)

U.S. chemical engineer Margaret Hutchinson Rousseau helped save thousands of lives. In the 1940s, she developed a way to manufacture the lifesaving antibiotic penicillin in large quantities, allowing much wider access to the drug. Rousseau had a wide range of interests and also helped develop a new kind of fuel for aircraft.

Penicillin mold is grown in labs to produce the antibiotic penicillin.

Civil engineer

This job is a good choice if you want to leave your mark on the world. Civil engineers can point at huge structures and say, "I built that." They work on some of the world's biggest engineering projects, from roads, tunnels, and bridges to airports and sewage plants. These are structures that may still be in use hundreds of years after they have been built.

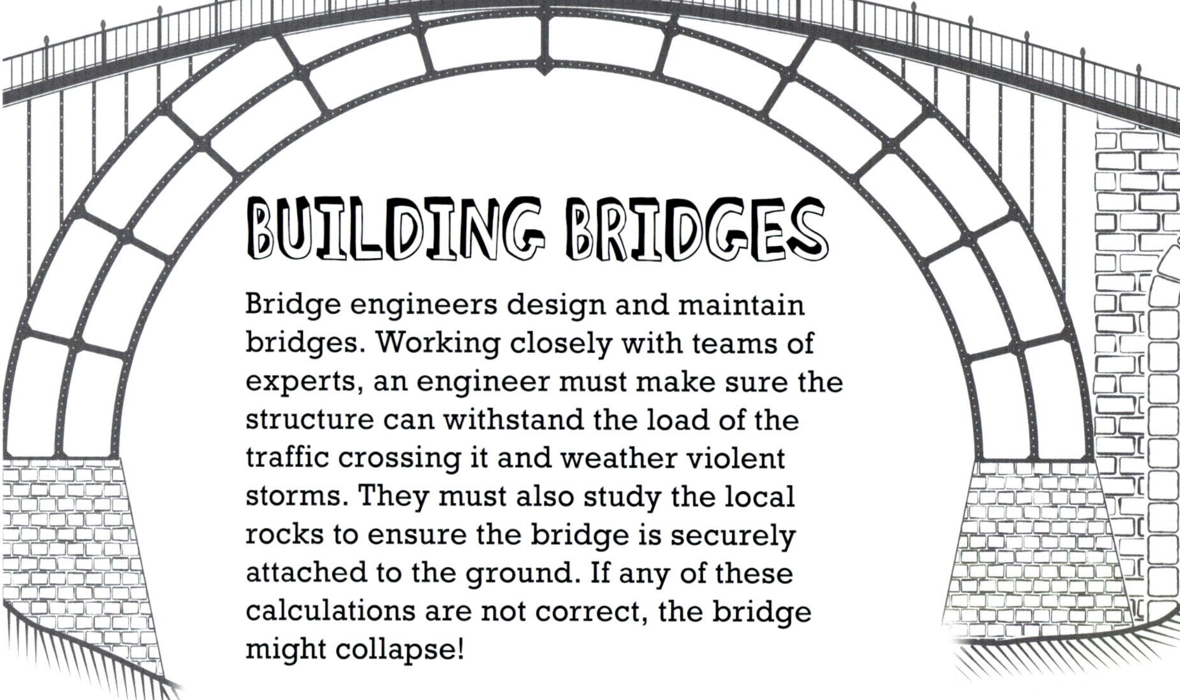

BUILDING BRIDGES

Bridge engineers design and maintain bridges. Working closely with teams of experts, an engineer must make sure the structure can withstand the load of the traffic crossing it and weather violent storms. They must also study the local rocks to ensure the bridge is securely attached to the ground. If any of these calculations are not correct, the bridge might collapse!

EARTHQUAKE ENGINEERS

In some parts of the world, such as Japan and California, violent earthquakes are frequent. Their effects on buildings can be disastrous. Earthquake engineers create structures that stand up to huge amounts of stress, although they can never be earthquake-proof. They test out their designs by placing them on shake tables. These large platforms jiggle around and can recreate the exact movements recorded during major earthquakes.

STEM STAR: GUSTAVE EIFFEL (1832–1923)

French engineer Gustave Eiffel is best known for building the Eiffel Tower in Paris, France, which was the tallest building in the world from 1889 to 1930. Eiffel also designed the internal support structure for the Statue of Liberty in New York City, which was created and built in France. Before these famous projects, Eiffel made his name designing bridges and stations for France's new railways.

Behind the scenes: Crossrail

Tunneling is an international career that could take you anywhere in the world. You'll be working on some of the biggest engineering projects of all. The Crossrail underground line (called the Elizabeth Line) in London, England, had a budget of nearly $24 billion! You'll need to like being underground, where you'll forge strong friendships and work closely with big teams of people with a wide range of skills.

Entire city blocks have been demolished to make way for the Crossrail.

TUNNEL ACADEMY

The Crossrail underground line has 26 miles (42 km) of tunnels. Many of the 12,000 people involved in the project trained at the Tunnelling and Underground Construction Academy, which was set up especially for the project.

Brand new stations have been built along some of the line's stops.

SECTION ENGINEER

Section engineers are responsible for planning the work on particular sections of a tunnel. You need to be very organized as you'll be managing a big team and handling a big budget. The machinery, materials, and people need to be in the right place at the right time to keep things running smoothly and on schedule.

TBMs

Tunnels are dug by giant tunnel boring machines (TBMs). The TBMs used for the Crossrail were 500 feet (150 m) long. They operated day and night for three years, moving through the earth and rock at 325 feet (100 m) per week. At the front of each TBM, a rotating cutter head sliced through the rock, which was taken away along a system of conveyor belts. Twenty-peoplc "tunnel gangs" operated the machines.

Inside one of the Crossrail tunnels during construction

A TBM uses a huge rotating cutting head to dig through the ground.

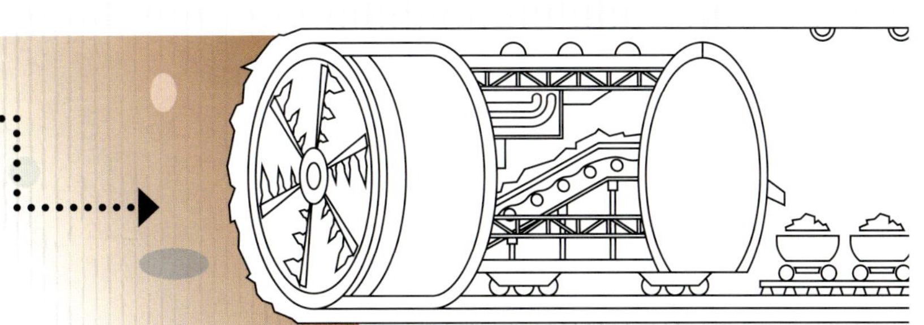

Dam engineer

Dams are built to hold back rivers or to stop the sea flooding coastal areas. They are also an important source of clean energy. As a dam engineer, your job is to build and maintain dams. There is likely to be a need for many more dam engineers in the years to come as our climate changes and the threat of flooding increases.

HYDROELECTRIC POWER

Some of the largest dams have been built to generate electricity. The dams create lakes behind them. Under huge pressure, water is forced from the lake through the bottom of the dam, driving turbines that generate the power. The Three Gorges Dam in China is the largest hydroelectric plant in the world. It generates enough electricity to provide power to more than 50 million homes.

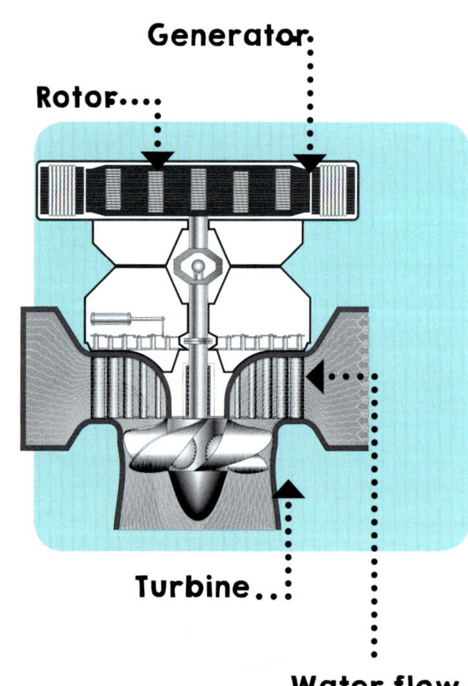

Flowing water spins turbines, which produce electricity as they spin inside a generator.

STEM STAR:
JOHN L. SAVAGE
(1879–1967)

American dam engineer John L. Savage worked on the designs for 60 major dams, including the Hoover Dam, a structure 726 feet (221 m) high built across the Colorado River in 1936. In the 1940s, Savage developed plans for a dam across the Yangtze River in China. His vision finally became real when the Three Gorges Dam was completed in 2012, but he did not live to see it.

FLOOD PROTECTION

While a dam has water on both sides, a dyke has dry land on one side of it and the sea on the other. In the Netherlands, much of the land is protected by dykes. The dykes prevent flooding on low-lying ground. Engineers monitor the dykes and fix any faults before the dyke breaks.

Dykes combine with natural features, such as marshes, to protect coasts from flooding.

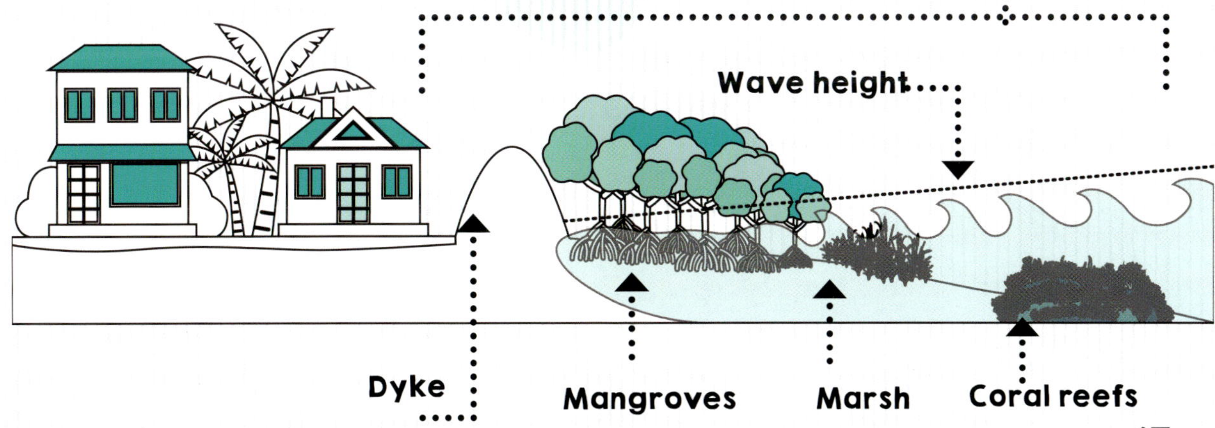

Mechanical engineer

When you're given a new gadget, do you feel the urge to take it apart to find out how it works? You might have the mind of a mechanical engineer. They build and maintain all kinds of machines, from cars and planes to elevators and air conditioning equipment. The skills you learn as a mechanical engineer can be put to a wide range of uses.

MECHANICAL MINDS

Mechanical engineers combine the skills of a scientist with the practical know-how of a mechanic. You need to get creative to come up with solutions for clever new pieces of machinery. Computer skills are also a must for creating and analyzing new designs.

STEM STAR: KARL BENZ (1844-1929)

In 1885, mechanical engineer Karl Benz built the first "horseless carriage" and called it the Benz Patent Motorwagon. It was powered by an engine that Benz designed himself and was the first automobile, or car, of its kind. It went on sale in 1888, but only had two gears and couldn't climb hills. It was Bertha Benz, Karl Benz's wife, who made the first long-distance journey by automobile in 1888 and suggested the addition of a third gear for climbing hills. She also invented brake pads on the way!

CLIMATE CONTROL

On planes, trains, and spacecraft, temperature control is vital, while laboratories need very precisely controlled environments, with exact temperatures and humidity levels. Keeping a stable environment ensures the results of experiments are as accurate as possible. Mechanical engineers create and maintain the systems that keep things just right.

Behind the scenes: Shipyard

The Sembawang Shipyard in Singapore has the largest dry dock in Asia. Here, some of the world's largest cruise ships are hauled out of the water for maintenance and refitting. A shipyard is a huge workplace. For large jobs at the Sembawang Shipyard, workers often live on site, riding bicycles to get quickly from one part of the dock to another.

SERVICING SHIPS

Ships must be taken out of the water every few years for a thorough service. Over the course of a couple of weeks, the ship is fully checked by teams of engineers. Marine engineers check the structure of the hull to ensure it is watertight, while electronics engineers test the radar equipment and steering.

A large cargo ship undergoes maintenance in the huge dry dock at the Sembawang Shipyard.

The *Voyager of the Seas* is more than 980 feet (300 m) long and can carry more than 3,000 passengers.

TOTAL REFIT

In 2014, Sembawang Shipyard gave the cruise ship *Voyager of the Seas* a complete refit. More than 3,000 workers spent 32 days completely gutting and rebuilding the ship. The luxury liner was fitted with virtual reality displays, a 3D movie theater, and an ice-skating rink. In total, the upgrade cost about $80 million.

SHIPYARD SAFETY

With heavy machinery, high work platforms and lots of deadly chemicals, shipyards are potentially dangerous places. Specialist engineers ensure the workplace is kept safe by regularly checking platforms and by providing technical training to those using machines.

Electrical engineer

We live in a world powered mostly by electricity. Engineers are needed wherever electricity is used, so electrical engineers can find themselves in a job almost anywhere: working on satellite communications systems, laying new lines, or developing new electrical products in a factory.

BIG AND SMALL

Electrical engineers could be working on medical equipment in a hospital or developing a communications system for a satellite. Or they might specialize in the growing field of micro-electronics, designing the electrical circuits in computers and smartphones. Wherever you find yourself, you'll need a good knowledge of physics, electronics, and electromagnetism.

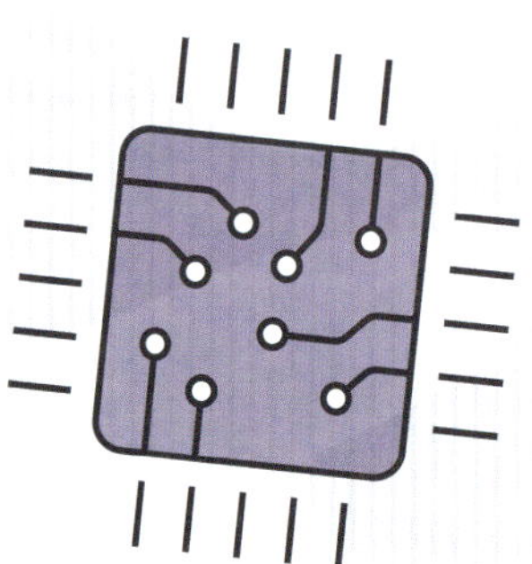

STEM STAR: NIKOLA TESLA
(1856–1943)

Serbian inventor and engineer Nikola Tesla was a pioneer in electrical engineering. He developed many new ideas in the 1880s and 1890s, including the system for transmitting electricity using alternating current (AC) that is still used today. Tesla also worked on ideas for radio communication, demonstrating its power by piloting the first-ever radio-controlled boat around a pool of water in New York.

POWER ENGINEER

Power engineers keep the electricity flowing. They build and maintain the systems that carry electricity from power stations to our homes: substations, lines, and pylons. Power engineers need to be prepared to deal with emergencies—when the power goes down in the middle of the night, you'll be the one called to fix the problem!

Computer engineer

Millions of people have a computer in their pockets in the form of a smartphone. Computer engineers work on all kinds of computers, from phones to powerful mainframes. There are even tiny computers in some ovens, TVs, and washing machines.

HARDWARE

Computer technology is developing at a breathtaking speed as computers become ever smaller and faster. This is all down to the ingenuity of hardware engineers, who are responsible for designing and building new computers. They develop and test new systems, such as processors, circuit boards, and memory sticks.

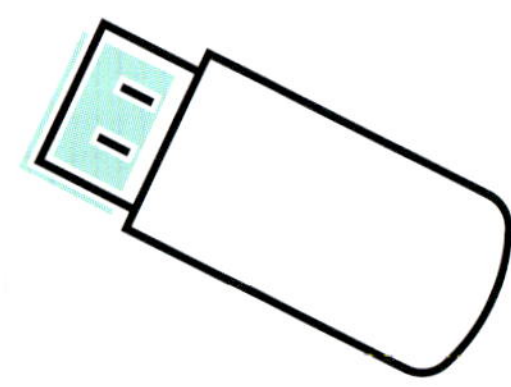

SOFTWARE

You cannot see the work that software engineers do, but without it, our computers would be totally useless. Software engineers develop programs and work closely with programmers to generate effective computer code. They combine engineering skills with computer knowledge to develop games, design new apps, or keep whole networks up and running.

Binary code

STEM STAR: TIM BERNERS-LEE (1955-)

Some engineers single-handedly change the world. Working at the CERN physics laboratory in Geneva, Switzerland, British software engineer Tim Berners-Lee came up with an idea to help scientists share information from their computers. He named it the World Wide Web (WWW). In 1991, Berners-Lee started the first website at CERN. Today, there are more than 1 billion websites, covering every conceivable topic.

Biomedical engineer

Biomedical engineers put their skills to work devising new forms of health care. This might mean making artificial body parts, building robotic surgery machines, or developing new advanced stem cell technology to grow new organs. As new technology becomes available, medicine is finding plenty of clever engineering solutions.

MIND CONTROL

Not long ago, when people lost an arm or hand in an accident, the best they could hope for was a hook to replace it. Today, engineers have developed robotic arms that are linked up to the person's nervous system. This allows them to control their artificial arms and hands with their thoughts.

Modern prosthetic limbs use ultra-lightweight materials to make them easy to control.

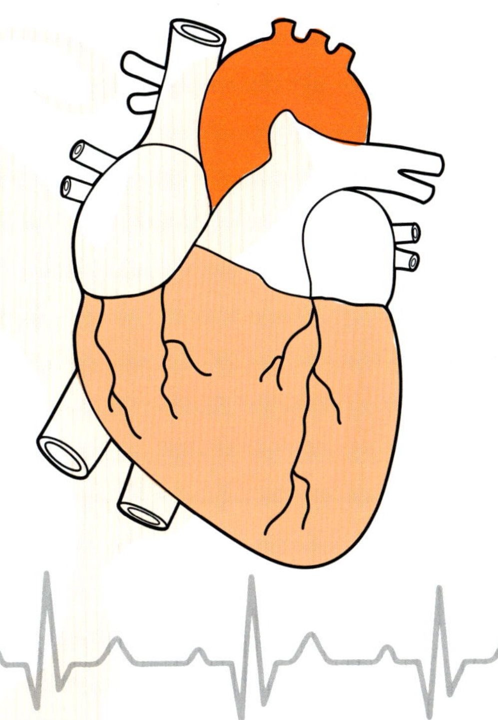

DIVERSE AREAS

Engineers work alongside scientists and doctors to create new treatments. They may use their knowledge of chemistry to create new drugs, or their computer know-how to develop software to run scanners, such as 3D X-ray machines. Some use their knowledge of mathematics to analyze the signals transmitted by hearts and brains. You might be working closely with patients or behind the scenes in a laboratory.

STEM STAR: YUAN-CHENG FUNG (1919- 2019)

Chinese-American Yuan-Cheng Fung had two successful careers. He started out as an aeronautics engineer, studying the way planes are stretched and squeezed during flight. Then, in the 1960s, he applied his knowledge of materials to the human body, pioneering the idea of "tissue engineering," treating patients with artificially grown tissues. Although he retired in 1991, Fung was still actively working on new ideas well into his 90s.

Behind the scenes: Nanoengineering

Are you fascinated by all the new things you see when you peer through a microscope? Nanoengineers work at such a tiny scale, making miniature machines that are only visible through a microscope. This is a job for someone who likes to pay attention to detail!

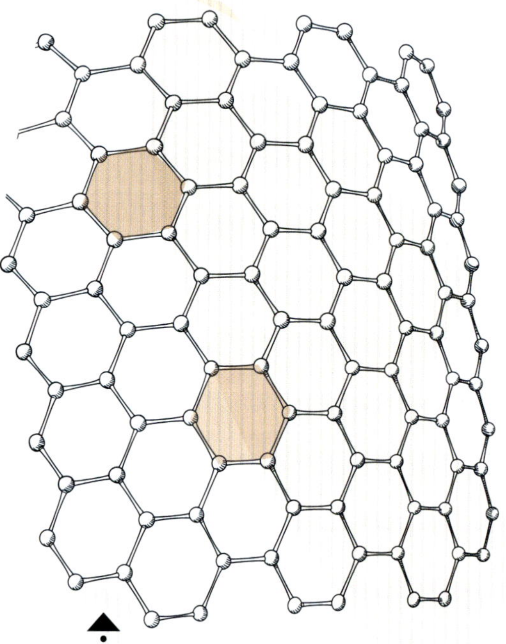

Graphene is a strong material that is made from layers of carbon, one atom thick.

STRONGER MATERIALS

Nanoengineers change the structure of materials at the smallest scale to make them much stronger at the large scale, creating building materials for bridges, buildings, and vehicles. By arranging individual molecules of carbon in a very precise way, nanoengineers have made a form of carbon called graphene that is stronger than steel. It is used to make fan blades for aircraft engines.

TINY STRUCTURES

Using 3D printing technology, it is now possible to build miniature machines. To demonstrate this, scientists at the University of Vienna, Austria, printed a racing car, complete with wheels and a streamlined body that was as wide as a human hair. It is also possible to print microscopic scaffolding that looks like the Eiffel Tower with trusses just 5 nanometers, or 5 billionths of a meter, across.

MINI MOTORS

Micromotors are tiny motors made to deliver medicine around human bodies. Doctors can guide the motors to just the right place using magnets. The tiniest motor ever made is less than a nanometer across. Small enough to fit inside a human cell, it can rotate at the same speed as a jet engine. It could be used to deliver targeted treatment that attacks cancer cells while leaving healthy cells alone.

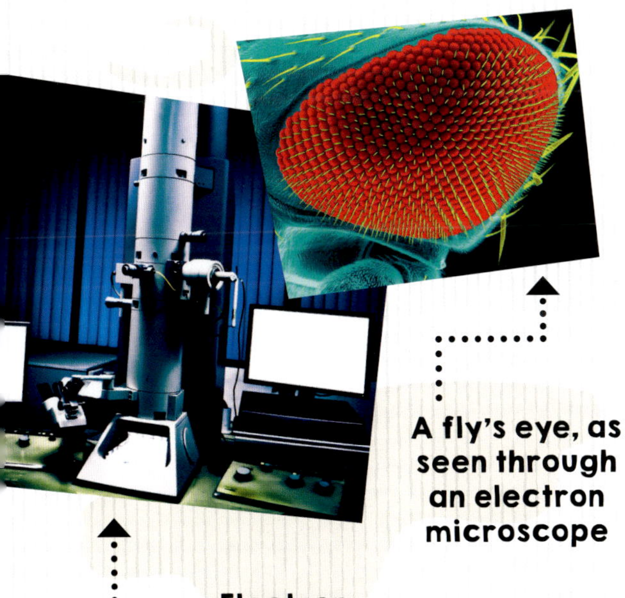

A fly's eye, as seen through an electron microscope

Electron microscope

SEEING SMALL

Microscopes that use light to see objects can only see down to a scale of millionths of a meter. Below that, the image becomes fuzzy, so a scanning electron microscope is needed instead. It fires a beam of tiny particles called electrons at objects and monitors how the electrons bounce back. In this way, it can see detail down to a scale of a nanometer.

Systems engineer

Do you like to take charge during games and come up with winning strategies? Some engineering projects are very complex and they need people like you who can oversee the whole thing. A systems engineer has usually trained in one area of engineering, but they need a wide range of knowledge of lots of different areas so that they can see the bigger picture.

INFORMATION TECHNOLOGY

Large companies depend on huge IT (information technology) systems, with many thousands of computers linked together in a network. Systems engineers design, build, and maintain the IT infrastructure to keep everything working smoothly and make sure the data is safe and secure. You'll be working on big projects with huge budgets—a large company seeking to modernize its IT may spend hundreds of millions to make sure they get it right.

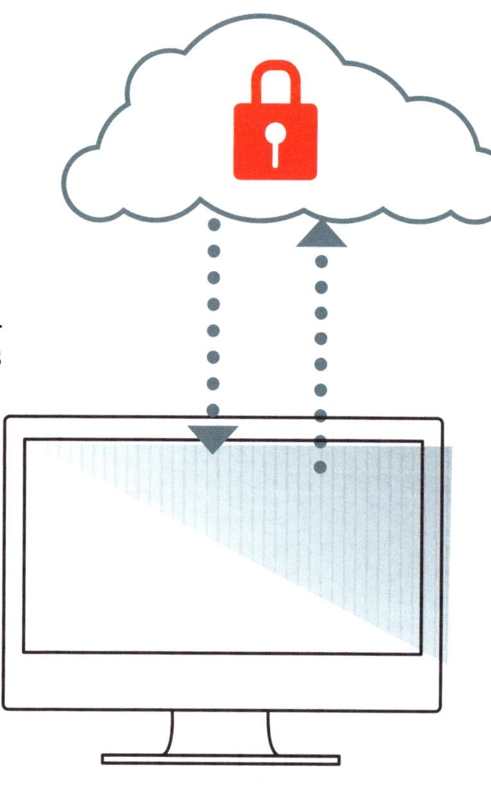

ROBOTICS SYSTEMS ENGINEER

Robots are very complex machines. To build and operate them involves expertise in areas such as electronics, computers, materials engineering, and mechanical engineering. Systems engineers make sure that robotic systems are working properly. They need strong computer programming skills to fix robots that are not behaving correctly.

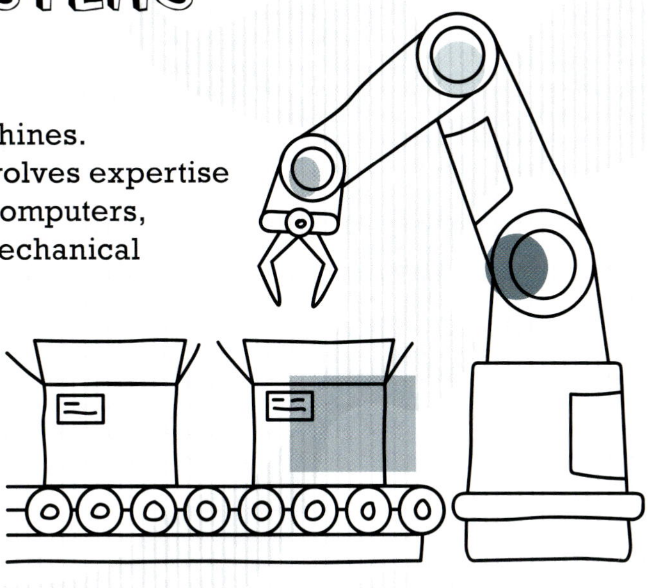

STEM STAR: GENE KRANZ (1933-)

Aerospace engineer Gene Kranz was in charge of one of the biggest engineering projects of all time—the Apollo program. As Flight Director, Kranz led Mission Control for the Apollo 11 mission that landed on the moon in 1969. The biggest test of his career came a year later when the Apollo 13 spacecraft suddenly lost power while in orbit around the moon. Kranz's team successfully guided the astronauts safely back to Earth.

Materials engineer

Do you find yourself testing new gadgets until they break, seeing just how far you can take them? Materials engineers develop and test new substances for manufacturing. These might be special heat-resistant materials for spacecraft or materials that can be used safely in medical devices.

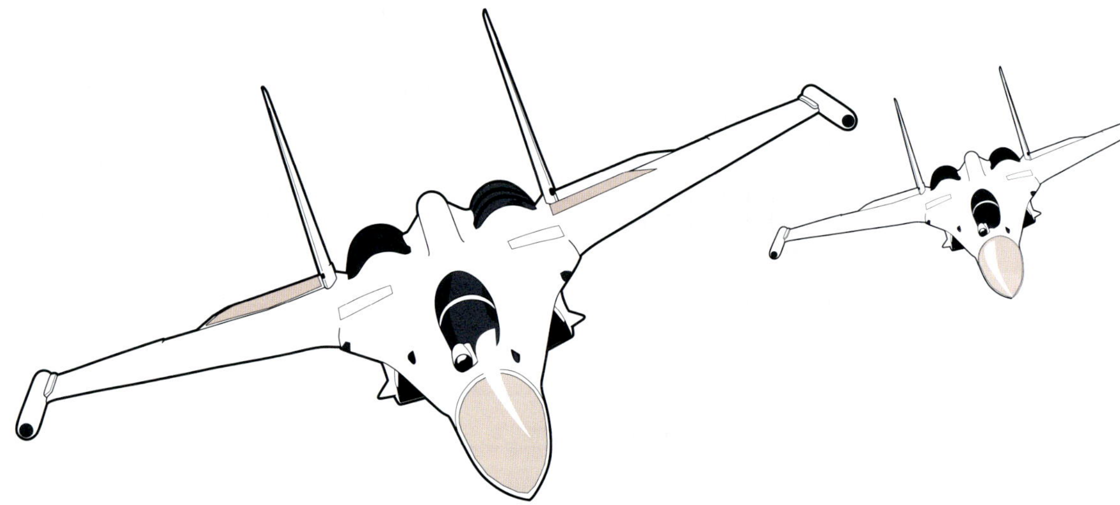

STRONG MATERIALS

Vehicles, such as aircraft and fast cars, need to be both very strong and as light as possible. Engineers have created new high-tech materials to make the bodies of aircraft and cars, such as carbon fiber reinforced plastic (CFRP). Extremely light but also very stiff, CFRP contains tiny strands of carbon, thinner than a human hair, which are woven together using special robotic looms.

STEM STAR: ALEXANDER PARKES (1813-1890)

If you look around, you can probably count dozens of objects in the room that are made of plastic. This flexible material can be molded into just about any shape. The first plastic was invented by British chemist Alexander Parkes. Made from a mixture of oils, cellulose, and alcohol, it was called Parkesine. Today, there are thousands of different kinds of plastic, each with different qualities.

Early movies were shot on celluloid film. Celluloid is a type of plastic.

MAKING SMART MATERIALS

Smart materials are substances that react to changes in their environment, such as when they are stretched or heated, or have electricity passed through them. Memory foam is a smart material that molds its shape around a warm body. Developed in the 1960s by materials engineers at NASA to make safer spacecraft seats, memory foam is now widely used in mattresses and cushions.

Memory foam can change shape under pressure, then return to its original form.

Metallurgist

Metallurgists are engineers who work with metal. More than 6,000 years ago, ancient engineers created the alloy bronze by mixing copper with tin. Since then we have discovered different metals and more ways to mix them. It can be exciting work, involving big machinery and molten metals at temperatures over 2,000 degrees Fahrenheit (1,100 degrees Celsius).

SEPARATING THE METALS

Metals are found in the ground around us in the form of ores. These are rocks that contain metal mixed with other minerals. Chemical metallurgists develop the best ways to extract the metal. They heat the ores to melt them, then use a variety of methods to separate the metal, such as zapping the ore with electricity or mixing it with other chemicals to create a reaction.

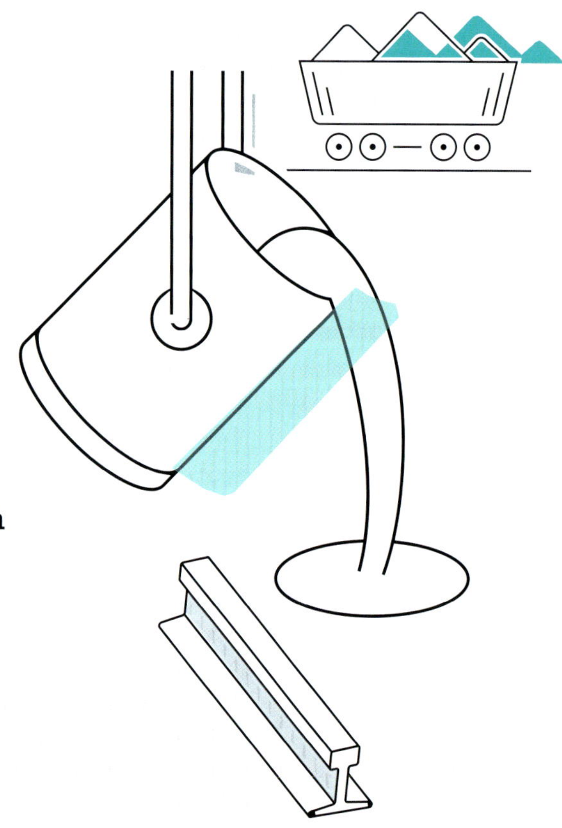

STEM STAR: HARRY BREARLEY (1871–1948)

Imagine eating soup with a rusty spoon! Before the 1920s, cutlery was made of silver, which did not rust but was very expensive. Steel cutlery was no good as it quickly became covered in rust. British metallurgist Harry Brearley solved the problem by inventing stainless steel—an alloy of iron that does not rust. Within a few years, affordable stainless steel cutlery was widely available.

SAFETY TESTING

Large structures, such as buildings or bridges, often depend on metal supports to stay upright. Physical metallurgists study the properties of metals, testing how they stand up to extreme pressures or weathering. They use their knowledge to check metal structures for weaknesses, so they can be fixed or replaced before an accident happens. If an accident does happen, metallurgists investigate to work out why the structure failed.

Petroleum engineer

Petroleum companies extract oil and natural gas from reservoirs deep underground. It is the engineer's job to work out the best way to drill into the reservoirs and force the oil or gas to the surface. As a petroleum engineer, you might find yourself in remote places, working with scientists and drilling crews on land or at sea.

OUT ON SITE

Drilling engineers supervise the drilling of a new well, making sure that it is done safely. Once that is done, production engineers take over to monitor the oil and gas production and fix any problems. A single well may stay in use for up to 20 years, but companies are constantly searching for new ones. You'll be traveling from place to place, keeping an eye on lots of different wells.

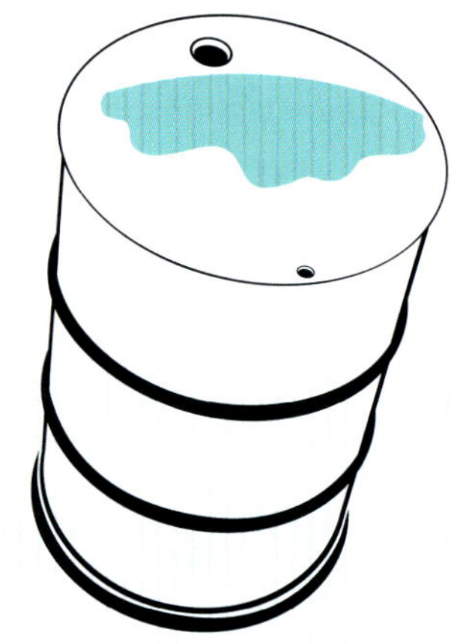

SOUND MAPS

Reservoir engineers study underground reservoirs. They produce maps of the reservoirs by firing sound waves at the rocks to measure how they bounce back. Using their knowledge of geology and chemistry, the engineers work out exactly how much oil or gas is down there. Each reservoir is different, so drill engineers need to get creative to find the best way to extract the fuel.

STEM STAR: LINDA COOK (1958-)

American businesswoman Linda Cook began her career at oil company Shell in 1980. Working as a reservoir engineer, Cook rose through the ranks to become the head of Shell Gas & Power. Today, she works for a company that funds new energy projects around the world.

Renewable energy engineer

If you want to help build a greener future, there is no better place to work than the renewable energy sector. You will be creating ways of generating electricity that do not pollute the planet. As we find ways to replace oil and gas as our main source of energy, this is a booming business that is only going to grow, so you should have plenty of work!

WIND ENERGY ENGINEER

Many wind energy engineers are scientists who design and test wind turbines, specializing in electrical, civil, or aerospace engineering. Others make sure turbines keep working properly. The turbines work best in the windiest areas, so you'll be on location in some very windy places and even at offshore wind farms.

SOLAR ENGINEER

Solar panels capture the energy of the sun and turn it into electricity. Solar energy technology has improved hugely in recent years, meaning that countries with cooler climates can also benefit from using solar panels. Engineers design and build solar energy projects, from huge commercial projects to home rooftop installations.

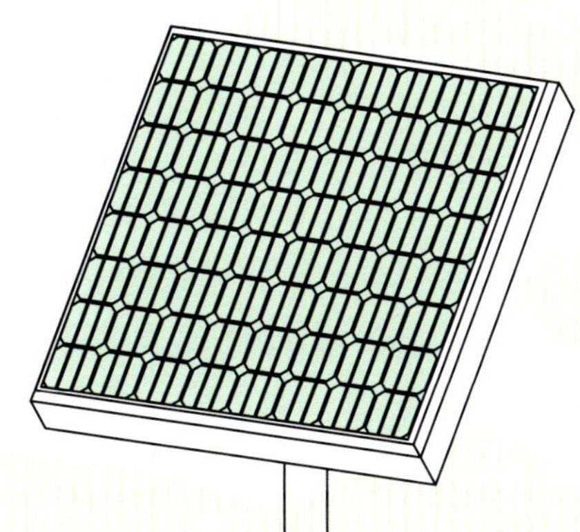

STEM STAR: PALMER COSSLETT PUTNAM (1900–1984)

American geologist Palmer Cosslett Putnam was the first person to think of using wind turbines to generate electricity. In 1941, he built a giant turbine that fed electricity directly into the grid—the first wind machine ever to do so. Putnam was a visionary who wrote about the importance of clean energy many decades before the idea became commonplace.

The first large-scale wind turbine, designed by Putnam

Behind the scenes: Geothermal power plant

A geothermal power plant taps into the immense energy right beneath our feet. It sends water through pipes deep underground, where it is warmed by hot rocks and turned into steam, which rushes back up to ground level like a geyser. The steam drives turbines to generate electricity.

ACTIVE ICELAND

Iceland is highly geologically active, meaning that it has lots of volcanoes, geysers, and natural hot springs. While there may be snow at ground level, very hot rocks lie just beneath the surface. About a quarter of Iceland's electricity is produced by geothermal power plants and all its homes are heated by them. The power plants have become popular among tourists, who can take a tour of the plant and enjoy a soak in one of Iceland's many hot springs.

The Blue Lagoon is part of a geothermal power plant in Iceland.

Geothermal engineers drill to test conditions underground.

SKILLED TEAMS

Scientists work alongside skilled technicians and craftspeople to build and maintain geothermal power plants. Geothermal engineers need to be experts in rocks, finding just the right place to drill down and tap into their energy. They also need to ensure that the drilling does not cause the ground to become unstable.

FINDING NEW LOCATIONS

As the technology improves, more and more places are being found where power plants can be made. Soon, geothermal power plants may be common around the world, not just in hotspots like Iceland. Unlike solar or wind energy, this is a source of energy that is constant, generating electricity 24 hours a day, every day of the year.

Design engineer

Are you always coming up with ideas for new gadgets? You could put your inventive mind to good use as a design engineer, developing products and manufacturing techniques. You'll need knowledge in a wide range of areas to take your ideas from the computer screen to the marketplace.

NEW DESIGNS

Today, new products are designed using computer-assisted engineering (CAE) software, and you'll spend hours tweaking your ideas on the computer before you make models for testing. You'll need to remain patient. British inventor James Dyson tried out more than 5,000 different designs for his new vacuum cleaner before finding the right one! Today, he sells his cleaners all over the world. Perseverance pays off.

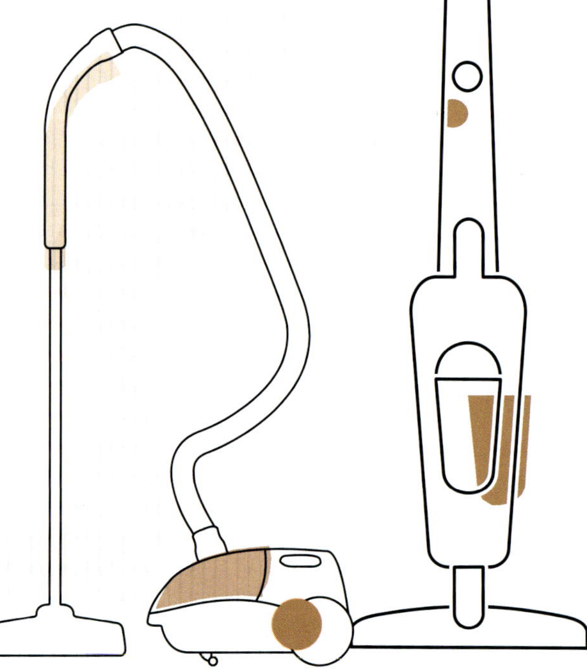

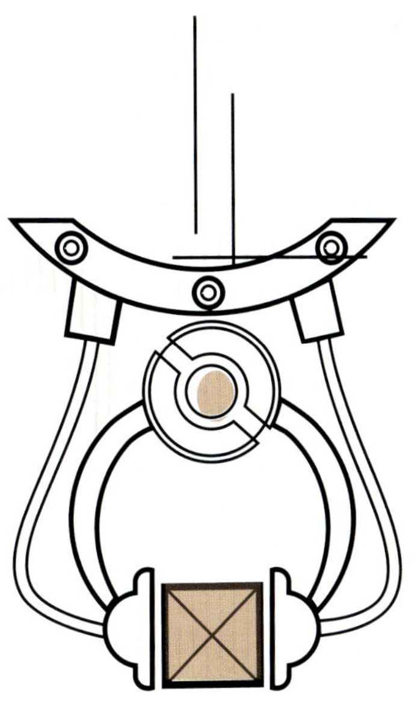

SOLVING PROBLEMS

Design engineers are often sent particular problems to solve. They need to make products that not only work well, but are also easy to make. You'll need knowledge of manufacturing so that you can tell factories how to make your product correctly and on budget. You'll also need to believe in yourself—before you can bring your idea to market, you have to sell it to your clients!

STEM STAR: NEETI KAILAS (1985-)

Indian industrial designer Neeti Kailas founded the Sohum Innovation Lab to develop ideas for affordable health care in crowded hospitals in the developing world. One of her most successful projects was a new low-cost method to screen babies for hearing loss, for which she won the 2014 Rolex Award for Enterprise.

Telecom engineer

Do you love climbing trees? You need a good head for heights as a telecom engineer, as you may be working on high overhead lines. You will be building, testing, and fixing telephone networks, satellite and digital TV technology, and fiber optic systems. Telecom engineers may have a degree in engineering, or they may have gone through an apprenticeship.

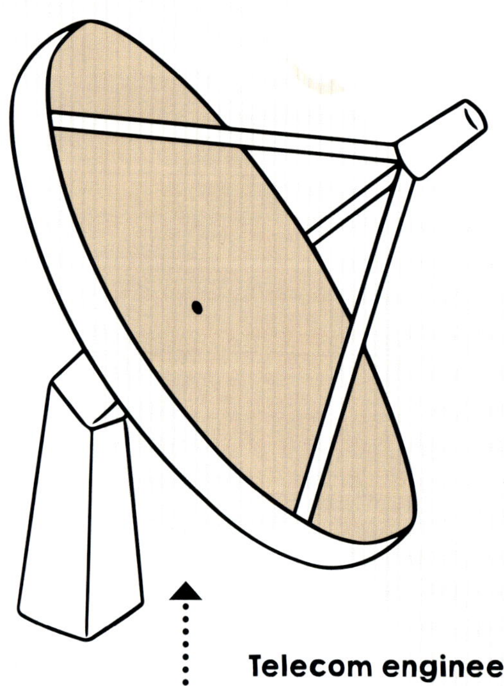

Telecom engineers install and repair telecom and satellite systems.

NEW TECHNOLOGY

Telecom technology is changing all the time, with ever-faster computers and high-tech lines. Engineers design and install new systems, making the world more connected than ever. You might be working in research and development or in technical support, but whatever field you're in, you'll be part of a team of skilled professionals.

STEM STAR:

CHARLES KUEN KAO

(1933-2018)

Chinese electrical engineer Charles Kuen Kao won a Nobel Prize for Physics in 2009 for his work on fiber optics. By combining glass fibers with lasers, Kao created a really quick way to transmit digital data. This led to the creation of the superfast broadband "digital highway" that makes the internet possible.

LEARNING ON THE JOB

Telecom engineering requires specialist skills, and you will never stop learning on the job. When you first start, you will often rotate between different areas, gaining practical skills both in the field and behind a computer. Jobs vary widely, and you might be working on a large business network one day and then a home satellite installation the next.

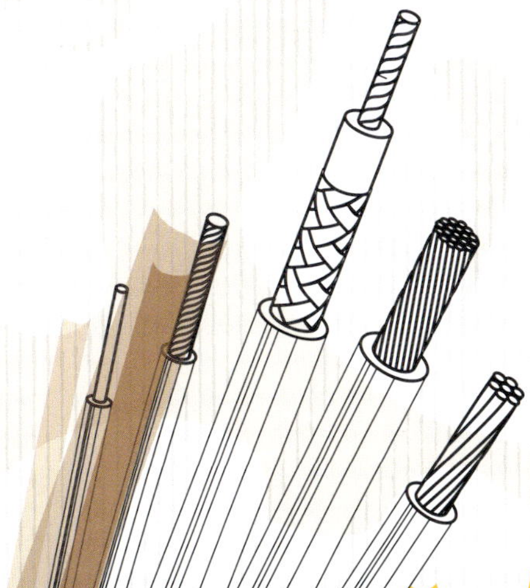

Glossary

alloy
two or more metals that have been mixed together

apprenticeship
a position that allows a person to learn a trade from a skilled employer, while earning a small wage

artificial
something that is made by humans and doesn't grow in nature

automobile
a vehicle that moves using its own power and is usually designed for passengers

autopilot
an automatic driving system that allows ships and aircraft to be controlled without human involvement

avionics
the science of electronics used in designing and making aircraft

cell
the tiny building blocks that make up all living things

circuit board
a base upon which electrical parts are joined together to make a working circuit, used in electrical devices

computer-aided design (CAD)
software that allows the use of computers to create technical illustrations of buildings and products

computer code
a set of commands that tell a computer what to do

drone
an unmanned remote-controlled aircraft, like a robot that flies

earthquake
the sudden movement of Earth's crust that can be felt over large areas

electron
a very small particle that orbits the nucleus of an atom

fiber optic
extremely thin fibers made of glass or plastic that are used to send information very fast

fuel
a substance that provides heat or power when it is burned

geology
the study of nonliving materials in Earth's crust, particularly rocks

geyser
a jet of hot water that erupts from underground, often creating hot springs

hull
the frame or body of a ship or boat

humidity
the amount of water vapor held in the air

International Space Station (ISS)
a large spacecraft and scientific laboratory that is in orbit around Earth. Astronauts live and work on the ISS.

loom
a machine used to weave individual threads together to create materials